MW01715418

Ovid at Fifteen

Christopher Bursk

New Issues Poetry & Prose

A Green Rose Book

New Issues Poetry & Prose
The College of Arts and Sciences
Western Michigan University
Kalamazoo, Michigan 49008

Copyright © 2003 by Christopher Bursk. All rights reserved.
Printed in the United States of America.

First Edition, 2003.

ISBN 1930974256 (paperbound)

Library of Congress Cataloging-in-Publication Data:
Bursk, Christopher
Ovid at Fifteen/Christopher Bursk
Library of Congress Control Number: 2002112915

Editors	Herbert Scott
	Jonathan Pugh
Art Director	Tricia Hennessy
Designer	Emilie Oswald
Production Manager	Paul Sizer
	The Design Center, Department of Art
	College of Fine Arts
	Western Michigan University

Ovid at Fifteen

Christopher Bursk

New Issues

Western Michigan University

Also by Christopher Bursk

Standing Watch
Little Harbor
Making Wings
Place of Residence
Places of Comfort, Places of Justice
The Way Water Rubs Stone
Cell Count
One True Religion
Working the Stacks

for George Drew, Cornelius Eady, Sandy Solomon, Betsy Sholl,
Joan Aleshire, and Pamela Perkins-Frederick,
whose poetry reminds us what matters

for Sy Safransky, Herb Perkins-Frederick, Helen Lawton Wilson,
Steve Pianka, Lloyd Winter, and Peter Bridge,
whose words dare us to imagine what is possible

and for Mary Ann, my children, and grandchildren,
whose love reminds me what matters and is possible

Contents

IV.

I.

Ovid at Fifteen

1.
Not another naked woman
sprouting roots,
the kid in front of you moans,
your classmates and you tired
of all those virgins
begging to be branches,
fountains, marble statues.
What red-blooded American
boy understands girls
named Byblis, Iphis,
Arcas? All those sisters
spinning till their hands turned
claws, their mouths
beaks? Arachne's nose
falling off, then her ears, and all
for art, one more woman shriveling
into a spider.
Maybe not the best story
for fifteen-year-olds
even if you're prodigies
in Latin. Medea, Medusa, Circe.
Jeez, this one's got snakes growing
out of her head,
this one's got dogs
where her cunt should be. Just
what you suspected:
women
are not what they seem.

2.
One minute, a girl's in love
with her brother, the next
she's a faucet
that can't be turned off,
and her brother's bathing,
in her, drinking her up. You'd think

these guys in myths would learn
to stay away from pools
after Actaeon was demoted
to a deer and devoured
just for looking
down into the pond
where a goddess, who'd come to swim
naked, was breaking
into ripples.
It's a boy's greatest fear,
his dogs turning on him,
his friends hot on his trail,
tracking him down and then feasting
on his raw flesh,
that outrageously
out-of-control, all-night stag party.

3.
Keep your trap shut.
If there's a moral
to the myths, it's: blab
and you're a boulder, boast
and one by one
your babies are turned into toads.
Keep your wishes to yourself
or you'll dine
on unchewable gold,
your breasts will be wrinkled
balloons. Don't even think
out loud
or you'll soon end up a statue
or a rat or a raven.
Too late to learn from your mistakes,
as you drive the family chariot
straight
into the sun.

4.
Harder to bend than a willow,
harder to move than a river,
as deaf as the sea.
What do fifteen-year-olds have
in common
with a centaur, his long-winded
wooing of a nymph,
simile
heaped upon simile,
as if he could wear down the girl
with the weight of his
elaborate tropes? Of course,
you and your friends laughed
at a fat, bearded man
in the body of a horse.
Like the maiden, you had your minds
on beauty
and what it'd be like
to be held by it,
not something old,
barbarically huge and sad,
and almost untranslatable.

5.
Suspirar, desnudarse, suffrir.
You're being marched
down a candlelit marble hall,
naked, martyred, your longings
turned elegant
in Latin
while your coach draws diagrams
on the board,
his voice so serious
he could be planning the sacking
of Troy. You're working
on your own book
of surprises. You're a vine.

You're dew
on the feet of young girls,
a field of daffodils.
Nymphs shrivel
into nothing but a voice
out of love for you.
Ganymede?
Hyacinth?
How does a boy explain
to his teammates
he longs to be so dazzling
a god couldn't resist him?
How does he tell his coach
he'd like to be ethereal,
a gold-fringed bird
with no obligations
except to wake the world?

6.
Screechings, shrills, squeaks,
tiny, dislodged
synonyms flinging themselves,
fur and claw, against the walls
of your skull,
radar gone haywire,
dislocations, near-collisions,
careenings, skiddings
across the air.
Of course you keep silent
when it's your turn
to recite for the teacher.
You love Latin too much
to trust its royal lineage
to mucus, spit, and speech,
the nominative's obedient
entourage: acquisitive,
eloquently senile genitive;
supercilious dative;
sorry-ass accusative,
that old belly

that always gets the spear;
and best of all,
the familiar
of grief and guilt, the ablative,
always modifying,
qualifying,
final e, faithful servant
that expects nothing
in return.

7.
One moment you're ordinary,
a son, a brother,
and the next
a god is finding you
so remarkable
there's no escape
except to turn into a tree.
And when you try to
speak, your voice
drops. It cannot push through
all those thick cells
of wood and water. Such work,
this turning all at once into
bark and leaf,
such effort devoted
to plumbing, to making sure
gravity relents
and water rises,
to digesting the sun, meal
after meal
of light, your arms tired already
of the weighty obligations
the air is determined
to hold you to.
Does wisteria appreciate
the tangle

light gets it into?
Do clematis, ivy, morning creeper
feel gratitude
for being lured up
a lattice, tricked, and left with nothing
more to grab onto?
Just try to
fall to your knees, beg
for mercy. Kill yourself?
Changed,
you're no more free
than a tree is. Like it,
you've got responsibilities.
You've got to hold up the sky,
take water
and light and air
and translate them,
leaf
by leaf—into what?

The Great Book of Bats

It's almost obscene,
the snout,
the entire head
jammed up the hole
till all that's visible
are the legs and the wings
trying to fly straight up
the funneled
flower, a creature
giving itself up
so completely
to sucking
the boy can't shut the book.
Hairy, slit-faced bat,
long-tongued bat.
dog-faced bat, snout-nosed bat.
Pages of them
like mugshots:
thumbless bat, large-footed
myotis, trumpet bat.
Solomon's naked-backed bat,
with froth on its face
and a gasp
of surprise. Leschenault's
rousette, Chinese pipistrelle,
Cuban fig-eating bat.
Australian ghost bat,
an entire planet of bats.
Here's the picture
the kid keeps
turning back to:
Philippine sable-winged
flying fox
plucks a frog in mid-
mating call
and bites
into its small song.

You're neither fish nor fowl

your mother likes to say,
meaning, *You're the age*
you don't know
what you want. Neither boy
Nor man.
Not male, not female.
You're always bumping into walls,
doors, trees, people,
as if your body's just sprouted
wings, and the world's more cramped
now. The feathers trail
along the ground. No matter
how many baths or showers,
you can never get clean.
In the mirror you lift
your arms and there's nothing
attached to them.
But when you dive off a rock
or pull yourself out of water—
what used to be
second nature—you're lifting
the whole pond with you, the trees
reflected there,
all that weight stitched
to your shoulders, the itch,
the rank odor
of rain dried into this fluttery
armor, an affliction of feathers
woven to you.
Breathe. Can't
breathe. Drown. Claw
at the sky. The air
like water.
The water over your head.

Your Father Sunbathing

Sundays, your father climbs out a window
onto the roof,
looking for somewhere
there are no women,
nothing else to do
but undress,
lie down and open his arms wide,
spread his legs
and make an X,
a target for the sun
to concentrate
all its energies on,
the groin, the seat of the soul, the
hairy, breathing sac,
and your father
summoning all the light he can,
his exhaustion
heroic, a warrior's.
What if you follow,
quiet as the light,
kneel
beside him, intimate
as the sun, trace his calves,
his ankle's spidery veins,
even his tired feet
cocked to one side?
Like someone blind,
you want to read the line
of your father's jaw,
the story of his mouth,
your mouth on his shoulders,
his belly—lightly
as you'd kiss a flower,
brushing your lips across
your father's
penis, its taste like
petals, wet grass, wax
candy, old dolls.
Like women at the cross

who gather the crucified
                    into their arms,
          stroking a miracle,
not to take the wound
                    away
          but to know
what suffering really is.
                    Mary,
          Mary Magdalene.
It seems so natural,
                    the mouth
          pressing against all
it's drawn to.

Saturday Night

You've let the cold run so long over each hand,
it fits you like a glove,
you can almost wear it away from the faucet.
For the lack of anything better to do
you've scrubbed your face too,
then let the washcloth's dark
fall over your eyes, your nose, your mouth.
Then another washcloth, then another,
their heavy animal sadness pressing against you
till their need feels as great as yours.
Another day of shooting hoops in the rain,
of walking a creek,
of keeping water company,
of envying even it,
preoccupied, as it always is, with the rocks
it wears grooves in, the trail
it keeps widening in the earth,
following the same path, never bored,
rubbing the day over and over.

The Matches

Hurt yourself. It's an idea that gets a boy out of bed,
looking for a matchbook,
lifting its cover and pushing it back
to reveal the small, hooded assembly huddled there.
They could be watching from the prow of a ship.
They could be a baptismal party wading in the river,
or a band of hostages
from whom a maiden is plucked
to be sacrificed, to blaze forth, her wild hair tossed back,
to die. The boy holds the match
to the back of his hand. Fire peels away the skin.
The skin shrivels as if there's not much to it, nothing
lasting. He presses the match head
down, its little ardency,
grinds it out—almost as if to punish the flame.
It's the sting afterwards he wants, proof
he's alive, in pain, and there's something he can do
to stop the pain: cause more.

The Weeping Lady, The Fallen Warrior

The Temple of Four Fathers—
I'd named the rocks
so they'd belong to no one
but the waves and me. No one else
came here, so I hadn't expected
to push through brambles
and find real men on my Altar Stone,
licking the sweat
off each other's shoulders,
arms, legs. Even the tops of their feet glistened.
It was like watching cats
clean each other, that odd moment
of tenderness between creatures
with claws. At first
I thought the one was going to
kill the other. I'd never seen a man kiss
another man, much less
press so close; he looked
as if he were trying to crawl
inside his friend. Afterwards
the two dove off the rocks
and though I saw no sign of a boat
they headed for the horizon
as if they meant to
swim the entire sea.
Their hands kept stabbing
the surface and it kept
healing over. I watched
till there was nothing left
to see, and for weeks after
I rode my bike back, hid in the weeds,
and on the Altar Rock
tried, alone,
what the two of them had done together,
as if the hands had gifts
I'd never fully tested
before and they might do
what the mind couldn't.
I told no one.
It was just one more secret between me

and stone,
me and sky.

So This Is Who You Are?

On the subway, a man
tips your head back
and looks straight
into your brain
as if you're hiding something
from him,
and to find it he's going to
tear you open
with his eyes. There are
levels to you
he plans to descend, dark
thoughts you never knew
you had. Then he's inside you
as far
as a man can get
by staring. You're a grave
he's robbing, a mine
to be ravaged of its ore.
It takes a long while
before your mouth can
make the shapes
of words again.

Icarus

Veer. *Swoop.*
Dive.
Plummet.
Plunge. The limited vocabulary
of longing.
When does knowing
that what he wants
is impossible
ever keep a boy
from wanting it? *Wings.*
Feathers.
Light. It's not the sun
that sends Icarus crashing,
but the weight
of all the ordinary
air on his shoulders, millions
of molecules,
the vulgar
facts of chemistry, jealousies
of physics.
It's not flight
he yearns for, as much as
the solicitude before
and after,
his father's hopes for his soaring,
his father's pity
for his fall, Daedalus
bending over Icarus
as if a boy's body
was meant for more
than just taking out the trash
or kicking a soccer ball,
the man's hands
on the boy's shoulder blades,
just under
the boy's arms,
stitching wings
to the wings
on the boy's back.

II.

Surprise the Muses, Take them by Surprise

I cannot match your fervor.
Nay, nor still the ache within
With any but white violets.
Nowhere in my school did anyone talk
like that. All morning
I thought about those violets
till the snow started to fall
with determined gentleness.
I'd never suspected.
Here, another language
besides the one my Dad spoke,
or my coach used
to whip the team into shape,
my teachers
to make us feel stupid.
The ancient theatrics
of noun and verb.
Their extravagances.
If your eyes had been blue
I'd have bartered and slaved,
lied and haggled,
and died for you. More
than one way to love:
the adjective's
seductive malingerings.
With marge of ice,
fire grass, white steel,
Syrian pink, jasper, cygnet. And then
a faucet running
somewhere in the house,
my brothers arguing baseball.
The cold
made me seem even more
naked, the air touching me
everywhere.
If your eyes had been gray,
I'd have worked out the chart
of the stars

for you.
I lay down with stunned obedience
as a child might
on an altar.

Blowjob

Spunk. Jism.
Cum.
You'd think it would smell
more remarkable,
given the effort
to call it out of the body.
But it's not that different
from watery tapioca
or warm club soda. Not a fact
a kid wants to admit
who'd like to think
he's risked everything
for it, and made it so obvious
the other kids in school
have no choice but to
torment him, push his face down
into the toilet
after he's boasted
how he picked up a few
of their fathers.
Want to guess whose
old man likes to suck dick?
he managed to
spit in their faces
as they yanked out his head
dripping.
What do you do
if your best friend throws away
all hope
of being normal, liked?
Here's your chance
to be martyred
too, give up everything
you've been taught
to work for,
turn in your uniform,
tell your teachers to get fucked.
But for what?
Hint

of vanilla, odor of old
paste, blunted sting
of salt?

The Word

To see what it looks like on paper, you print it
in block letters, draw it out
like a breath, make it roll over the page like a wave
cresting. Try different scripts,
write it over and over
as another young man might
the name of the girl he dreams of marrying.
The pleasures of the language,
of shaping a secret thought into sounds
and these sounds into letters,
a word set all by itself on the page
spread out before you like a map,
an island too exotic and distant to hope to reach
right now. Even after you rip up the page,
tearing even the smallest pieces smaller
in case someone reads your trash,
you repeat the word. In school.
During lacrosse practice. Deep in your mind
you are casting a spell,
creating a small charmed circle around yourself,
etching a line no one can cross.

Top Shelf

A boy has to drag a stool all the way down the aisle
to the back of the news store
and then balance on top of it
if he wishes to see the tattooed ladies
perching on motorcycles,
gymnasts
astonishing their limbs into inextricable
positions, muscle men gazing up
from the pages
as if they had expected this very boy
to come to this very store
and step onto the footstool.
He almost has to leave his feet
to reach them, his arms
thrust out a little further
than arms are meant to go. Only the tips
of his toes keep him
from falling. He stretches
for what he isn't sure he wants, bodies
polished like expensive furniture
or racehorses,
thoroughbreds rubbed down, each day,
so huge and sleek
he imagines them pawing the ground,
blowing smoke out their nostrils,
rocking the sides of stalls,
their immense muscles, powerful
gears of a machine left running.
He slips a magazine
under his shirt;
inside it are kids
just as skinny as he is,
on their bellies, on their knees,
pale and exhausted. They must have been wandering
for days. They look younger
than the eighteen years
the magazines claim they are.
A man is resting his hand
on a youth's shoulder,
his other arm lifted to the kid's face.
He is turning the boy's head

perhaps to kiss him,
perhaps simply to
offer directions,
set the lad on his way.

How far did you get?

Often the first question
other boys hit a boy with
as if he hadn't merely gone on a date
but had tried to
swim the English channel
and they knew he couldn't
cross such a distance
without their help
and this was their way
of helping—*Go on,*
tell us exactly how far—
interested in measurements,
how often, how long,
the precise calculations
of sex. What is a kid to reply?
It was like
grabbing hold of a boat,
being pulled aboard
after treading water for days.
I lay there
as if I'd been rescued,
looking up at the stars
as if they'd been part
of the search party too,
the breezes on my neck,
the whole dark sky.
That might be more
than his buddies
wanted to know.

Swept Overboard Again

Please, you're hurting me!
One man holds you down.
Another thrusts himself inside you.
It's as you imagine drowning,
the ocean with its colossal hungers.
I'm sorry, I'm sorry.
You wake next to a young woman
you decide right then you'll marry.
Her hand brushes lightly over your damaged body,
your nipples, your belly, the tip of your penis.
It's like being made love to
by rain, warm
summer rain. Afterwards
even your pores seem wiser.
But always in the place between dreams
and waking, there are the men
like rocks water has just drawn back from.

New Year's Eve

Your girl wanted the two of you to be even more naked,
so she held out a gift, her first of the New Year,
a small leather day-book with gold-leafed pages
just like the one she'd bought for herself.
At either end of the sofa,
the two of you were to write down everything
you'd not been able to say.
At first you didn't know what to fill the pages with,
so you scribbled what you thought
she'd like to hear, your suicide attempt
at thirteen, what it had felt like
to peel away your uniform after a game,
what you had hoped for,
alone, lying on the roof,
and then you were writing what you hadn't expected
and then reading her eyes
as she read what you'd tried to slur,
one word rushed into another, penmanship
so awful maybe she'd get tired
of puzzling out your confession, secrets
you had thought you would die with, the truth
that would turn her from you
finally. Not because she knew it. But because
afterwards you'd ask if it made a difference
and keep asking till it did.

779.24

My fingers chose the book,
not my eyes. On page 176
a young man, draped
over a chair, was fabric
begging to be
unfolded. On page 213
he lolled on a couch like a courtesan.
On the next page,
his penis sprawled over one leg
the way a hobo loafs, his sack
of worldly possessions
thrown down.
In one picture the photographer was naked too,
playing a flute
as if he'd felt left out. He too
wanted to be touched
intimately
by the light.
Why did I feel compelled
to check the notes
for the model's name?
It was mine. My grandfather's.
Right age. Right city.
Who was he, this man
who'd walked my brother
and me to our first haircut,
who'd fallen asleep
listening to ball games,
and smelled of licorice
and pipe tobacco,
and made us recite the names of capitals
before he let us have ice cream?
This same man at nineteen
let his clothes fall to the studio floor
as if his body hadn't belonged
only to him, pale throat, erect nipples,
belly so round, it seems now
the most naked part
of him. No waistcoat, no vest,

no silk scarf. Nothing between
the one undressing
for the picture
and the one taking it
but the camera promising
the only comfort it knows.
You're no one's son,
no one's father.
Just curve and line,
one more place
for shadows to gather.

Rorschach Test

It seems like a trick, the man
pulling a card out of the deck
and placing it before the boy.
If the boy sees a woman's groin,
it's a spider. A hand splayed out
is a gang
dividing to get away from the cops,
a river breaking into tributaries.
What is unmistakably a penis
is a walking stick.
He knows he's supposed to talk
and so he talks. The dark wings
are a boy's jacket spread wide
and trying to fly.
And that tall figure is either a tree
or an old man watching
a girl hang from the end of a kite's tail.
It is lifting her away,
and before she knows she'll not be able to
let go. It'll be no good screaming,
she'll be swept too high for anyone to hear.
And then the doctor
puts the cards away and asks the boy what he did
when the man loosened his belt.
Did nothing. Said nothing. Pretended
to be too tired
to notice. He was an old man dying,
a tree
someone was twisting a piece of fruit off,
a branch snapped in two.
Nothing could touch him.
Okay, imagine you are a tree now,
the doctor says, resting his hand
on his patient's arm.
What does it feel like?
Like nothing, the boy says.

What a Boy Does Not Say

Of course I gave in.
I was fifteen.
On the nape of my neck,
the small of my back,
many flames,
all with one purpose.
Then he was fire
that could pass through
any closed door.
I almost believed
I'd been entered
by light itself, a prince
who'd undressed me
as if I were the only country
he wished to rule.
How could I button the shirt
I'd worn yesterday,
zip up the pants
my mother bought me,
tie my shoes, grab my homework,
catch the bus,
later, at football practice,
endure the ordinary
crashing of one body against
another, the common
nakedness of boys
in the shower,
the little blood washing off,
missed blocks,
interceptions, a day's
minor conquests?

Ovid, Book III

The gods are so busy, so good
at ruining lives,
we forget that
they can't get to everyone
all at once. Fate can
only do so much. It can't
see that absolutely all cars
crash, all planes
slide off the runway,
every storm
gets its chance
at every ship.
Every village has to take its turn
being leveled.
every microbe must wait
for the right opportunity
to devour a man's flesh.
This is a tale
told often: a boy
marked for the worst
kind of humiliation
and spared
at the last moment.
Out of mercy?
Perhaps. An oversight?
Maybe. Or just boredom?
The gods get tired
of turning men
into pigs or flowers.
Sure, the boy was
raped, but just by a man,
and the man
let the boy go
as no god would.

III.

Midas

No winesap apple, no Chinese pear,
no bell pepper.
Nothing polished. No
blueberries with the dew still on them,
none of the raspberries'
chiseled sweetness.
Long after the gods took pity,
he still expected the peach
to break his molars.
Muscadine, Persian melon, muskmelon—
eating these
would be like sinking his teeth
into ingots. Even after the gods
took back
their cruel gift,
he suspected a trick. How often
do gods repent?
It didn't matter
that they'd changed their minds,
did it, Uncle Midas?
After an accident
you still hear the crash
years later, metal
on metal, and still
you lift bodies out from under
the tires.
Having done the unthinkable
it's all you can think about,
even if
your old life's restored.
Boozy old numbskull,
you're not the only one
to ask for something
stupid and get it.

Swallow

A quick buoyant meal,
    a small capsule, the size
of one of those jumping beans
    a kid pushes over
so it'll bounce back, a wobbly army
    that won't
stay balanced. One pill a day
    to teach the nerves
a new way to feel, the doctor
    insists. A little
plastic coating. The dry pod
    of a dead insect.
Open it and it's a packet of dust,
    of sand
that's inhabited a shell
    for centuries.
Just try it! a father pleads.
    What's wrong
with being happy?
    a mother wants
to know. Inside the capsule
    just enough
sugar for a doll's teacup,
    the pinch of arsenic
inside an apple seed. Dry ice
    of a witch's lips, kiss
of everlasting sleep. Shake
    the powder onto
your waiting tongue. It won't
    refuse any feast
offered it, no matter
    how small,
how familiar. *For once*
    do as you're told!
The doctor leans forward.
    Trust me, he says,
holding out the capsule,
    pale green of winter
apples, ivory
    of old dolls.

There's Blood on Those Grapes

One moment he's just a kid getting out of his car
in front of a supermarket and the next
a small dark man is lifting the picture of a corpse
over his head. The boy learns to walk
by pushing the dead body away, letting it
fall back against his legs. He could be wearing a skirt,
the sandwich board's that long. A few kids snicker.
A father shakes his head and hurries his children past,
their hands sticky with hot-cross buns.
A girl from French class pretends not to notice
that a murdered farm worker is hanging from his neck.
Jesus, Jesus. The boy says his name over and over
till it belongs on his lips.
There's blood on those grapes!
The picket line's not a bad place for a boy
to learn the power of words. *Motherfuckers!*
he shouts as the cops wedge him in the patrol car
with the old Filipino jammed beside him.
At least we're off our feet for a while;
be quiet, boy, scolds Mr. Encarnacion,
who once turned 200 cars away from a store,
who can still persuade a shopper
that her fruit salad will be the ruin of Western Civilization.
Don't you worry about Jesus.
He lifts his hand to the now torn photograph.
Jesus, my old friend, never looked better.
Released from jail, the boy's back, panting after leaflets
that have blown out of his hand,
pursuing them across the parking lot,
his sandwich board bouncing against his knees.
To think a klutz like you could change the world!
Once more, old Encarnacion chuckles,
resting his hand on the boy's shoulder,
that welcomed burden.
What good are words
if you don't chase them a little?

Taking to the Streets

Leave your eyes alone. Let me help you.
A kid's grabbing my hands,
pulling them away from my face,
a boy not much younger than I am, the age of the students
I've started to teach, all of us eligible
for the same war. Out of the fog,
the National Guard rise in waves.
This kid's prepared. With one hand
he holds my face still;
with the other he dabs petroleum jelly on my cheeks,
my forehead, and rubs it in,
fingers running over my eyelids so lightly
I, who cannot bear to have my eyes touched,
do not pull away.

**

At first we'd moved so close to the soldiers
it'd been fun: almost
like letting waves nip our ankles and then fleeing
and circling back, a sort of teasing,
give and take, all afternoon. Most of us hadn't expected
the attack dogs, gas masks,
a phalanx rushing in like a tide that gives no warning.
It was like trying to run in water
up to the waist. Gas everywhere, the thud
of clubbed bodies falling. An elderly man buried his head
in his hands and not till I knelt and pleaded
did he finally get up and try to escape.
A dazed girl clung to the fence. I pulled her fingers loose.
And all the while I kept wishing I could talk to my father
as if I wasn't a father myself,
and it wasn't my job now
to make sense of the world. I'd get to a phone,
like a news correspondent, report to my Dad,
that man who had believed everything
could be solved by words, their tireless
negotiations. Maybe now I'd get him to listen,
see how much of what he'd taught me was wrong,
as if somehow his admitting this
might make an ocean relent

and apologize. Sorry, it was
truly sorry for having used its great authority
heedlessly, all these years.

* *

One cop flings me to the wall.
The other yanks my arm back so hard it's obvious
it's not enough for him
to subdue me, he's going to make me never
forget. All I can do
is twist around to glare at him. Staring.
That's my only weapon, remembering his face.
All my life, my father's faith has risen above me,
a shimmering, impregnable edifice
with no doors to beat against, no windows
to shatter, a view so lofty
it acknowledges nothing but mountains,
skyscrapers, stars,
its equals. Not a son taking deep breaths
before he's hit, someone
the police have to teach a lesson.
A third cop brings down his club
on my shoulders, my head
again and again, in the same measured way
my father used to hammer,
making sure the nail was driven home.

Old Glory

In front of my students I start tearing out the stitches
so everyone sees the frayed edges of their flag
folded over and sewn out of sight.
I've never been able to leave things alone.
My friends and I used to break those Fourth of July flags
given us by the Veterans' Post, snap them in two
for spears, daggers, gold bullets
from the flags' sawed-off caps.
It's just cloth, this flag I hold to the light.
We gaze through its thousands of many windows.
No single color. No whole cloth.
Instead a thing woven as much out of what isn't part of it
as out of what is. Air.
Light. The match held to a corner seems to
hesitate, weigh the consequences
as if the flag had a choice
whether or not to let the flame seize hold of it.
Then it gives in to its manifest destiny
and the whole United States of America is burning
in a silver bowl. Ashes
lighter than any of us would have imagined,
like the feathers of a dead bird,
with the same soft folds.
My students and I pick out the threads
of a few stripes, the tips
of a few stars
none of us has the heart to throw away.

MWF, 11-11:50 a.m.

I'm all right now, I'm back on my meds,
says the prim girl
majoring in labor relations.
The prom queen's
a recovering coke addict and
mother of two.
The wrestler's father killed himself.
It takes a while
before the faces get attached to
what they write,
the pronoun error
to a short stay
in a reformatory, the subject-verb
disagreement
to a passion for hockey.
The Hindu point guard
is running for tax collector
on the Libertarian ticket.
The outfielder denies plagiarizing
an essay in favor of
radical feminism. *What do you know*
of my life? Of my mother's?
The elfin boy with rings
in both his nipples
(he pulls up his shirt to show us)
is pre-med.
The pony-tailed girl writes
her process analysis
on three steps to successfully smuggling
dope into jail.
The kid in a wheelchair
goes forward
backwards, pushing off
with his feet
and singing show tunes
down the hall.
As soon as he sits down,
the baby-faced boy

in the motorcycle jacket
                    shuts his eyes.
There are no dreams
                    like those dreamt
in the late morning sunlight
                    that falls through
a classroom window.

Will this be on the test?

asks the girl
with the tiny diamond in her nose
and when the answer's no
she closes her book.
Her silly teacher's
perched on the back of his chair
like a bird chirping
to the branches
as if they cared.
So she writes in the margins
of her copy of *Hamlet*
her boyfriend's name,
Frederick
Frederick
Frederick
till it's unexpectedly
foreign. Last night
she looked in the mirror
and saw another face,
someone she wasn't sure of
anymore. She looks up,
the teacher's still talking.
Ophelia.
She writes down the name
and then she's in a garden
right after the rain,
the flowers wet to her touch.
Ophelia. Why is she so sad,
suddenly forlorn?
She writes that word
too. *Forlorn.* It pleases
and scares her.
Why does she feel
the earth shift in its orbit
as if it'll never be
righted again, the world
all at once
tilt?

The Personal Essay

Afterwards hed always buy me
Ice cream.
Pistacchio. I'd go into a rage
if he suggested another flavor.
I was eight.
Hed drive and drive
till we found a stand
that sold
just what I wanted.
Today her words rush
onto the page
like water bounding
out of a pipe, delighted
to be free
of such tight quarters.
Not chocolate Not vanilla. Pistacchio.
It sounded foreign,
tasted grown up.
Maybe his hands did go
where they shouldn't
but thats not
what I remember. I remember
how even after
I got done with the cone
I could still lick Pistacchio
for hours
off my fingers.
Its the best I can do,
she ends her essay.
Is this what
you're looking for?
And though
she still can't spell,
after an entire semester,
tell the difference
between its and it's,
it is, her teacher thinks.
And it isn't.

Why You Find So Many A's on My Class Roster

Sorry, says the mother of five, a church organist.
She didn't have time to re-type her essay.
Her husband wasn't going to let her make a fool of herself
again, he said, so
with red pen he'd X-ed through whole paragraphs
of what she'd written, all the metaphors
she'd delighted in,
that sounded like keys touched lightly.

Yesterday, the 7-11 clerk tore his research paper into pieces
right in front of the whole class.
La Belle Dam Sans Merci, my ass! People are starving
and you want me to redo my footnotes?

The waitress dashes in late.
Last night her apartment was broken into.
Her nine-year-old called the police.
They had to take away his father in handcuffs.
Can I try the test tomorrow? she says in a rush
as if, somewhere at her back,
there's still a customer waiting.

The man with the impeccably groomed silver hair
is grateful for any class
where he's allowed to revise. His essay's not due
till next week, but he'd like to start now,
is not quite sure what's meant by critical analysis.
He's no hair stylist, he says,
but a barber. *Come by and I'll give you a trim.*
He likes having a teacher with unruly hair
and young enough to be his son.

His own boy died three years ago
of AIDS. *I didn't know he was a homo-*
sexual. He pronounces the word
as if it were one he'd just read in a book
and still had to sound out.
I didn't even know he was dying.
That's what hurt. That my son hadn't told me.

That's what I can't forgive Kevin.
He says his son's name
as if it were Latin for a rare flower
and the flower's beauty distilled in that one word.

Teacher Evaluation

What did I imagine?
That I could surround myself with girls
moving with the same ease

as water, boys
as unselfconscious as a brook,
and as impatient,

and not yearn to pull one close,
stroke another's cheek,
let my arm circle a third's waist,

draw the whole class against me
as a person might, in a light rain,
want suddenly to gather all the drops together

in his arms, press
out of all the separate glistenings of rain
one shimmering body?

Caessus

At a baptism, this god's already
preparing the infant
for acne,
braces, long afternoons
of bad television, lovers
who will break his heart,
the murder of boys
who like to dress up
as girls, the abduction
of girls who imagine it's okay
to open a door
and walk outside.
Lynchings, pogroms, massacres—
everyone guaranteed
their fair share
of misery, a cup of hemlock,
a cross heavy enough
for them to stagger
under its weight. Plant a seed
and this god's already
weeping for the drought
coming. He's condemned
to suffer
each winter bulb's
clenched hope, the ache
of every flower
trying to grow
in bad soil. Long before
they're hatched
he's digging graves
for the baby birds.

Teaching the Myth of Pelops to Ninth Graders

You'd think that if you'd been chopped up,
boiled in a cauldron,
served up to the gods by your father, the king,
you'd stay away
from royal dinners thereafter—that is,
if you were lucky enough
to be pieced back together.
The more I get caught up
with the idea, the more restless
the kids. One zips
and unzips his book bag,
another reties his shoes.
Athena just poked with her fork,
Juno complained
that the knee joint had too much gristle,
Hades pushed back and forth
the tongue on his plate. The penis
was rubbery as a chicken neck
so even Aphrodite wouldn't chew it.
It was fortunate
the gods didn't have an appetite that day.
I look at my charges.
They're waiting for me to get to the point.
That's a teacher's job
in fifty minutes or less:
to make sense
of a war, math problem, dismemberment.
What career do you suggest?
Carpentry? Accounting?
How's the boy to decide?
Probably he's too busy testing
his body, trying it
to see if it'll hold up. Once more,
like so many teachers,
I'm starting to tell my class more
than I'd intended.
Do we ever learn? Even Pelops' son
fricasseed his brother's kids.
The dinner table once again,

boys and girls,
the seat of a family's neurosis.
The House of Atreus:
ample proof of the virtues
of masturbation.

IV.

Big Nose Relegated: *The Tristia*

Boohoo, boohoo, no one speaks Latin here
and the weather's bad.
I want to come home. One more letter
from Publius Ovidius Naso,
as if no one's ever been exiled
before, had to learn
a new tongue, cook himself supper,
wear a knife
to bed, laugh at others' jokes,
so he'd not be killed.
Look, we all have jobs
and yours is
to take your punishment
like a Roman.
His friend does not write this back.
Instead, he lies
that he's arguing Big Nose's case
before the emperor.
Like a spoiled child on a rainy day
carrying on
as if he'll be the first to die
of nothing to do,
Publius pleads for the tides to go out
far enough
so he might walk back to Rome.
Bad water. Bad food.
Bad dreams. Even the disgraceful state
of his bowels.
The old poet won't take a hint and
shut up, all those dactyls,
elegiac couplets, futile
attempts to figure out
exactly what went wrong
and when.
As if a man has a right to
go on and on
about what's happened to him,
trying to

make sense of it all,
and to sing
and sing till it does.

The Note

At first it looks like a poem,
words darkening the page
like a messenger
pushing through snow,
crossing a battlefield.
To bring what?
A demand for surrender?
Terms of a treaty?
Sweet death, come swiftly!
Lines my father put down
in his own hand
as a teenager might—
no secretary, no typewriter now,
just slanted letters feverishly
rushing to their destination
as if the writer were the only one
ever to suffer,
words set apart on the page
as someone else might place a sculpture
on a pedestal
or a flowering plant by a window
so it could get the light it deserved—
as if the best reason
to put anything down on paper
was that you loved it—*Astrolabe, delphinium,*
grail, solitude, frisson.
If words couldn't
persuade a sweet, troubled man
not to pour another whiskey,
swallow another fistful of pills,
what were they worth? If I turn away
from the words now
and then turn back,
they are nomads crossing a field,
a restless, disheveled army
of veterans, dark figures
who wandered into a clearing
and, huddled there,

look almost harmless,
pausing once more
on their long migration.

Flight Lessons

When I found my father naked in the street
he looked like a boy caught
sleepwalking, tangled in branches,
dew on his face.
As a child, I'd fall asleep
to the speeches of soldiers
outside the walls of Troy, the creaking
of a great horse.
Homer had been his first tutor,
my dad used to say,
but Vergil had taken him
under his wing, taught him to fly.
I thought he really meant it
and pictured my father
wearing nothing but wings, Vergil
with his hand
on my father's shoulders,
explaining aerodynamics,
my dad poised for flight, a single shaft
on a bow drawn taut.
Now when I come home from a meeting,
an afternoon in court,
and take my father's hand, he lets out a breath
so deep
it's as if a door's been opened
in a room shut all day,
the air rushing out. My favorite passage
in *The Aeneid*
is when the hero, knowing the city can't be saved,
slings his father over his back,
carries him right through the walls of flame
and, once outside Troy,
rearranges this kindling back
into flesh and bone.
In the picture from my high school Latin text,
Anchises is perched
on Aeneas' shoulder, riding there
like a boy on his way to his bath,
an old man so light

he'd not slow down any journey,
a small burden the son barely feels.

Home Care

Let go, I beg, and uncurl my father's
fingers. He won't
drop his hand from the bed rail.
Help me, I ask and he does, finally,
let me roll him to the side,
loosen the tape of his briefs, loosen also
with warm water (but not too
warm—I test it, arm up to the elbow
as I'd do with my children's baths)
the dried fecal matter, wash it
from my father's inner thigh, peeling it
off the scrotum, lifting and scrubbing
(but not too hard),
at each step rinsing the cloth,
letting it fall back around the fingers,
so I can probe through it
the folds of the testicles, the little tucks
of skin around the penis.
Now it's smeared with the dark clay
of his shit, a reminder that he's not done
living. He's asleep now.
Hardly awake myself, I change his bedclothes, diapers.
Wanting all that touches my father
to be spotless, to smell of aloe and baby powder,
I pull over him a newly washed nightshirt,
and, under him, slip a sheet I've let air all day,
so he'll take in the fragrance of his beloved clematis,
the cold sea air
he once was able to breathe so easily.
Just as I used to with my son and daughter,
I bend down and kiss his brow,
as close to another man's dreams as I can get.

O Beauty, Fugitive Beauty

What am I to do with all the poems
where my father had implored beauty
to reveal herself, addressed her
gallantly like a jilted lover, rebuked her sharply?
Hundreds of heroic couplets
willed to me, a language so fired and faceted
he might have been cutting diamonds.
An ache that is buoyant fire.
Fire in my heart and head.
An ache that will never tire until I be dead.
A man imagines his affliction
a ship he is captain of, a mighty galleon
he's sailing out of the harbor
past the bell buoys at their thankless chores,
the farthest beacons,
long years, widening latitudes.
The waves may rise before him like the cliffs,
but he'll climb them,
the sky may fill with lamentations, but he will weep louder.
If the lightning throws itself in his path
he will thrust it aside,
steer his entire crew safely home.
Suffering is a boat just large enough for one,
a patched-up centerboard,
a single sail, a difficult crossing.

Compromising Pictures

My friends and I used to threaten to bring shovels
and dig our way in, beat off whatever small animal was living
on the sandwich you had laid aside
to find that one paper you needed
buried under the thousands you didn't,
shelves full of pamphlets, *Facing the Challenge of the New Prayer Book, The Doxology Revisited,*
opera ticket stubs, a jar of marbles, the bones
of a deer's spinal column, a cigar box of protest buttons,
now almost impossible for us to throw away,
even the smallest scrap of your handwriting,
draft after draft of an Easter poem left unfinished.

And finally all those pictures
wedged under so many issues of *Church Weekly*
no one would think to find them there.
Girls turning their faces to the window,
boys wrestling on the floor of sunlit rooms,
photographs torn out of magazines,
none suspicious by itself,
but taken together, proof of a terrible longing.
Children with skin the white of milkweed
stepping out of their clothes,
looking as if their bones were full of air.

Maybe you hid these pictures
not just so they wouldn't be found
but so they wouldn't lift away,
as if this was why you'd taken orders too,
put on robes, something heavy and dark
to weigh you down, to hold you
to one place, this life you'd been given.

A shout woke you one night—a shriek, really,
from your parents' room. You were nine
and couldn't figure out what it was.
Like something falling from a very high place,
that split second a person sees the world
is opening under him. When you searched the house

all you found were your father and mother
sleeping. They'd heard nothing.
You were imagining things,
they scolded. But you'd heard the soul
rising out of a person and you were sure it was loose
in the house. Listening, you stayed up till dawn.
Years later, you pulled me close to the bed
to tell me this story,
one of those a man offers to explain what he can't explain.
Here is my life, I know now
you were saying. *Here is all I have to give you.*

At the edge of a jetty a youth stands by himself.
He is lifting his clasped hands over his head
as if he's just awakened
and is stretching, offering himself to the morning.
You must have cut the picture out of a magazine
and unfolded it again and again.
What the eye is drawn to, first,
is the pale skin just under the kid's arms,
the little glint of each rib,
each distinct and glistening hair of his body.
The youth is covered in light
as if the sun had traveled millions of miles
only to stroke the curve of his throat,
the slope of his shoulders,
this boy, its inevitable conclusion.

April Fools

My son stops raking, straightens my jacket,
brushes the hair out of my eyes,
as if it's his job to see that I look respectable,
he and I cleaning out under the bushes,
scratching down to the wet black leaves covering the yard,
giving the grass a chance to breathe again.
Spring has come once more
despite the winds' best efforts to keep it away. It's easier
to let the flowers die, the trees pull
into themselves. *All that from a few cuttings,*
my son says, peering into the forsythia
he'd planted just a year ago, breaking off a few branches
and shoving them into the soft ground
as if to say, *Okay, now it's up to you.*
Now he shakes his head, as a father might
scold, *See, I told you. Will you never learn?*
The daffodils have survived the late snow,
as have most of the tulips
whose bulbs we buried last year,
my son's idea, his faith
not mine, his hands in the dirt.
I just held the bulbs out to him
as, years ago, I did with tools for my dad,
his head stuck into a car engine, every Saturday.
My son tucked the bulbs into their dark bed,
whispering the way a parent might
to coax his kid into the water.
It's okay. It'll be okay.
Even the dogwood is budding,
the one I'd told my boy wouldn't last the winter.
Don't get your hopes up too high.
But who was I protecting, scared even now
to let my eyes take in all these blossoms unfolding,
each petal's nakedness?

Watcher from Balcony and Bridge

Once
it might have been an honorable
profession, a strict code
of behavior required, training
more rigorous
than the priesthood: to stare
at a girl about to dive
till your muscles tense too,
till you feel the spring
in your legs. To gaze
at the back of a shirtless boy,
looking for wings.
Think of the discipline
it takes to live in the garden
and not to pick
what blossoms there,
to cherish the fruit
too much to rob the tree.
Willowy boy, shy girl,
God's kiss on your brow.
Who better
to drink the health of bride and groom
than the one who began
grieving for them
when they were five or six,
who studied how light fell
on their faces,
who worshipped kneecap
and elbow,
even the tiny pursed mouth
of the anus,
scholar of all the creases and folds
of a child's body?
Restraint? Nowadays
it's not a gift
many are taught
to be proud of.
To cock the gun but never fire?
Stabbed,
never to pull the sword out?
To make a living

out of aching. A solitary
                    and barely extant
vocation.

779.2A, 779.5B, 779.M48 . . .

My hands trail over books
                as if my fingers could read
        on their own—
physics, metaphysics, metalinguistics.
                I always start
        with good intentions
but all at once I'm back
                where I usually end up:
        in the bordellos and tenements
of the 770s, steerage crammed
                with refugees. Midgets,
        contortionists, cross-dressers—
I am touching everyone:
                children in masks,
        couples in doorways,
women in fake furs,
                a girl on a bicycle,
        the rippled abdomen
of a boy about to dive, the calf
                of each leg, every tensed muscle
        as if my fingertips intend to
take in not just the boy
                and his pond and the trees in it,
        but every road in and out of town,
the circus, the field of stones,
                the Union Army, the train tracks,
        the subway, New York's entire
East Side. The transvestite daring me
                to look away.
        The twins holding hands.
A boy with a cap gun.
                A girl in a wheelchair
        on a balcony. I have to touch
the curve of her neck, the light
                she brushes vigorously
        into her long, dark hair.
Some kinds of reading require
                the whole body.
        The hands have to
see for themselves. The fingers believe
                they know better

than the eyes
how to read.

Because the Eyes Are Not the Hands

A boy wriggling out of his bathing trunks.
    The soft webs of a girl's toes.
A gull swallowing a starfish,
    disc, madreporite, anus and all.
The silver-green crust of pipes.
    Mold, maggots,
worms after a rain (nothing more naked).
    A raccoon, that roadside bloom
opening till it's nothing but a seed pod
    of bones. That impertinent flower,
an old man's penis. What the hands consider
    off limits,
the eyes probe, their just compensation
    for not being fingers. Of course,
the eyes can't have what they want.
    Open a book of pornography
and try to hold your gaze
    to one picture. Soon you'll begin
turning the pages, as if this next one
    or thc onc aftcr
could well hold a body so perfect
    you'll never have to search
again. A boy's on a ledge,
    gazing out across the mountains,
seriously considering stepping off
    into the sky, that dizziness
the eye loosens in us, its lack of
    perspective—as if it's got a right
to everything: glistening bellies, throats,
    cars the pale gold
of the most expensive champagne,
    valleys so verdant
there are more shades of green
    than in a gardener's dictionary,
a sea so darkly turquoise
    it's not enough
to gaze down at the water.
    You want to throw yourself
off the cliff, plunge
    into the very heart of color.

Brave Vowels, Feckless Consonants

A girl's reading, the sun
filling the page
with its medieval text.
A boy's pulling off his shirt,
his back so smooth
it hurts not to touch it,
the hand once again
not trusting the eye
to tell the whole truth.
Two kids, stripped
to undershorts,
plunge into a pond
and come up, each time
empty-handed
and laughing, as if
that's the whole point: to keep
looking.
If you can't have
what you want,
at least you can
ache for it.
A kid's on a bicycle.
A bird's
darting back and forth,
mending a tear
only it can see
in the sky.

Aristaeus, the Son Never Talked About

One day he's humming
to his bees,
doing what he was born to do,
and the next day
his hive's dead
and he's wrestling with a weasel.
No matter what form Proteus takes,
boar or rat
or head full of snakes,
the boy hangs on
till the god has no choice
but to be wise.
Slaughter a cow a day
and stand watch
over the carcasses.
Aristaeus is no dummy:
he knows cures
often sound crazy
so he does what he's told
and kills cow after cow
till on the ninth day
out of the ninth beast's entrails
spills a great swarm of bees.
To celebrate,
Aristaeus puts out trays of sugar water,
sees to the small, essential details
of his paradise. A boy with honey
always on his hands?
People expect more
from the son of Apollo.
Not a kid with a tin ear,
a bad case of acne
and no aptitude
for archery. Bees hover
around Aristaeus
like cats waiting to be fed.
They perch on his arms
as if he's a shrub.
If a bee stings him
it's a compliment. Maybe
there's courage

in not being brilliant,
in doing the same thing
over and over,
walking familiar grounds
and taking delight
in what alights there.

Acknowledgments

Thanks to the editors of the following magazines, in which these poems originally appeared, some in different versions:

Another Chicago Magazine: "Ovid at Fifteen" (winner of the 2001 *Another Chicago Magazine* Award; published under the name Kip Irwin)

Anything That Moves: "Your Father Sunbathing" (as "Thinking the Forbidden")

College English: "Why I Give So Many A's on My Class Roster"

Comstock Review: "Swallow"

Controlled Burn: "Old Glory," *"There's Blood on Those Grapes"*

The Ledge: "April Fools"

Manhattan Review: "777.B4," "Rorschach Test," "Icarus"

North American Review: "Home Care"

The Sow River Review: "You're neither fish nor fowl"

The Sun: "O Beauty, Fugitive Beauty," "How far did you get?" "Saturday Night"

Some of the poems in this book were first published by Bacchae Press, in the chapbook *Working the Stacks*. They also appear in *Manthology: Poems of the Male Experience,* edited by Roger Weingarten and Craig Crist-Evans, and on the Word Works website.

The author wishes to express his particular gratitude to Herb Scott and his New Issues colleagues, Robert Brown of the Bacchae Press, Andrew Snee of *The Sun,* Gerry LaFemina of *Controlled Burn,* and Phil Fried of *The Manhattan Review;* and, for their faith in the enterprise of art, to the Spring Workshop, the Warren Wilson and Vermont College MFA Low-Residency Programs, the Vermont College Post-Graduate Writers Conference, and the PEW Foundation;

and to VITA (Volunteers in Teaching Alternatives), to whom the Green Rose Prize has been donated.

photo by Frank Pronesti

Christopher Bursk, the author of six books and three chapbooks, has been a recipient of Guggenheim, National Endowment for the Arts, and PEW Fellowships. He teaches at Bucks County Community College, and has worked for over two decades for VITA, a volunteer decision-making program within the correctional system of Bucks County.

New Issues Poetry & Prose

Editor, Herbert Scott

Vito Aiuto, *Self-Portrait as Jerry Quarry*
James Armstrong, *Monument In A Summer Hat*
Claire Bateman, *Clumsy*
Michael Burkard, *Pennsylvania Collection Agency*
Christopher Bursk, *Ovid at Fifteen*
Anthony Butts, Fifth Season
Anthony Butts, *Little Low Heaven*
Kevin Cantwell, *Something Black in the Green Part of Your Eye*
Gladys Cardiff, *A Bare Unpainted Table*
Kevin Clark, *In the Evening of No Warning*
Jim Daniels, *Night with Drive-By Shooting Stars*
Joseph Featherstone, *Brace's Cove*
Lisa Fishman, *The Deep Heart's Core Is a Suitcase*
Robert Grunst, *The Smallest Bird in North America*
Paul Guest, *The Resurrection of the Body and the Ruin of the World*
Robert Haight, *Emergences and Spinner Falls*
Mark Halperin, *Time as Distance*
Myronn Hardy, *Approaching the Center*
Edward Haworth Hoeppner, *Rain Through High Windows*
Cynthia Hogue, *Flux*
Janet Kauffman, *Rot* (fiction)
Josie Kearns, *New Numbers*
Maurice Kilwein Guevara, *Autobiography of So-and-so: Poems in Prose*
Ruth Ellen Kocher, *When the Moon Knows You're Wandering*
Steve Langan, *Freezing*
Lance Larsen, *Erasable Walls*
David Dodd Lee, *Downsides of Fish Culture*
Deanne Lundin, *The Ginseng Hunter's Notebook*
Joy Manesiotis, *They Sing to Her Bones*
Sarah Mangold, *Household Mechanics*
David Marlatt, *A Hog Slaughtering Woman*
Gretchen Mattox, *Goodnight Architecture*
Paula McLain, *Less of Her*
Sarah Messer, *Bandit Letters*
Malena Mörling, *Ocean Avenue*
Julie Moulds, *The Woman with a Cubed Head*
Gerald Murnane, *The Plains* (fiction)
Marsha de la O, *Black Hope*
C. Mikal Oness, *Water Becomes Bone*
Elizabeth Powell, *The Republic of Self*
Margaret Rabb, *Granite Dives*
Rebecca Reynolds, *Daughter of the Hangnail; The Bovine Two-Step*

Martha Rhodes, *Perfect Disappearance*
Beth Roberts, *Brief Moral History in Blue*
John Rybicki, *Traveling at High Speeds*
Mary Ann Samyn, *Inside the Yellow Dress*
Mark Scott, *Tactile Values*
Martha Serpas, *Côte Blanche*
Diane Seuss-Brakeman, *It Blows You Hollow*
Elaine Sexton, *Sleuth*
Marc Sheehan, *Greatest Hits*
Sarah Jane Smith, *No Thanks—and Other Stories* (fiction)
Phillip Sterling, *Mutual Shores*
Angela Sorby, *Distance Learning*
Russell Thorburn, *Approximate Desire*
Rodney Torreson, *A Breathable Light*
Robert VanderMolen, *Breath*
Martin Walls, *Small Human Detail in Care of National Trust*
Patricia Jabbeh Wesley, *Before the Palm Could Bloom: Poems of Africa*